A Good Book
Is the
Best of Friends

A Good Book
Is the
Best of Friends

A Reader's Journal

Robin Doak

Introduction by Natalie Goldberg

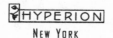
HYPERION

NEW YORK

Library of Congress Cataloging-in-Publication Data

ISBN: 0-7868-6719-1

A Creative Media Applications Production

Book design by Ruth Lee

FIRST EDITION

10 9 8 7 6 5 4 3 2 1

Table of Contents

Introduction

I have lived a whole, rich, and sometimes wild life, but I can clearly say that reading a book is still one of my deepest pleasures. It is something that human beings are meant to do—think about it: ants don't read; neither do elephants, whales, or field mice. It is a human endeavor, so why not delight in it to the full? First there are the words on the page—when we read the vowels carry our breath, then the consonants chop breath down to measured syllables. Whole orchestrated lines! What really do authors pass on anyway? but their breath at moments of inspiration.

But, Natalie, you say, I'm reading silently in my bed, at a cafe table with the rain hitting the pavement outside, under a sycamore in late summer, at the kitchen table while I wait for the water to boil so I can toss in the noodles. I'm not reading aloud.

Yes, yes, I understand. But even then our brain is breathing, our mind is living in Italy, the Sahara desert, we are battling invading armies, having black tea with Einstein or weeping over the loss of a child.

Where did you discover the book you are reading right now? A friend's recommendation? Wandering alone in a bookstore? You heard the author on the radio? To read a book is to enter into a relationship. How did it begin, how did it happen? We are careful to relish the meeting of a lover. He said. . . . She said. . . . But what about this book in front of us? How many times did you bump into it before you stepped into it?

I just completed reading *Desert Solitaire* by Edward Abbey. I'm a little embarrassed to admit that. Living in the Southwest for twenty-five years, being an environmentalist myself and even on the board of a nature organization, I've heard Abbey's name batted around so much I think I began to believe I'd read the book. I may have even lied a few times, "Oh, sure, yeah, it's a great one." But only now at age fifty-two, living in a tiny one-bedroom in an old brick apartment house at the corner of a busy street in St. Paul, do I open the book each night before bed and read about my Southwest. How did I come to do it?

I was visiting my old friend Vicki Pollard in Maine. We hadn't seen each other in three years. She had a terrible cold and couldn't leave the couch. She had just returned from the Canyonlands National Park in Utah and was raving about her trip. I have always known Vicki to be enthusiastic, but she's got good taste—so when she raves, I listen. She pointed to the bookshelf. "Over there, a video on Edward Abbey. There was only one at the park headquarters. You've read *Desert Solitaire*?"

I nodded. (Another lie on the same book. I would burn in hell because of that man.)

Vicki continued, "As I walked to the cash register, even the park ranger nodded. 'Oh, you've got a good one there.'" She sighed. "Natalie, you have to watch it."

I was leaving that afternoon, headed for my cousin's in Newton, Massachusetts. I promised to send it back within three days. She even had me sign an affidavit—we made it up on a sheet of loose-leaf paper. "I, N.G., swear with my heart and all the blood in me . . ."

At my cousin's I came down with Vicki's cold and sniffled and slept. I did not watch the film, but as soon as I arrived home I slipped the cassette immediately into the video machine. My partner watched it with me. It was OK—Edward Abbey was a bit macho. I didn't get it. Vicki never steered me wrong.

My partner said, "Nat, you didn't read the book. If you had, you'd be moved by the video."

Vicki called the next day. "Where's my tape?"

I laughed. "It's in the mail—I sent it this morning."

"Well, did you love it?"

"Oh yeah," I lied—I was headed for hell's bottom rung.

Enough! I had to read it. My partner, of course, had it on her bookshelf. OK, what was the big deal anyway? I sat down on the couch.

Two months later I'm still reading it. I read it slow. I want it to last. He wrote it when he was only twenty-three. He loves the desert and he opens that empty, big space for me night after night as I sit in this sweet slow Midwestern town.

I wish I'd had *A Good Book Is the Best of Friends* a long time ago. Think of all the pleasure I could have captured, like vacation snapshots, in this reader's journal, relishing the meeting of an author's mind and the deep journey through a book. This journal gives the reader the opportunity to have double pleasure like a double latte: Not only do you get to read a book, but then you get to savor the taste, roll it around in your mouth, and feel its complete flavor.

How To Use This Book

*T*his journal is a private place to record your thoughts and feelings about books that spark curiosity, challenge emotions, and provoke spirited discussion. The details you add to each journal page create a special reminder of the extraordinary people you meet and the places you go simply by reading a variety of books. This journal, combined with your love of reading, will guide your journey as you examine and shape your personal beliefs.

Table of Contents

The first part of the journal is the blank Table of Contents at the beginning of the book. Fill in this page with the names of your books. Information about your first book becomes Chapter 1 of your journal, information about your second book becomes Chapter 2, and so forth.

Getting Started

There are six pages to record information for each book. The first page is for pertinent information: the author's name, publication date, genre, and other data. Space also is provided to write a brief summary of the book's plot and major characters. Rating the book might be a good way to start a discussion. You can create your own rating system, or you can use the one provided here. (You may want to write your ratings in pencil—your opinion of a book may change greatly after you discuss it with friends.)

★★★★★   A classic! I would recommend it to everyone and anyone!

★★★★   Nearly perfect. I might make a few minor changes, but I would easily recommend this to a friend.

★★★   A good read. People who enjoy books in this genre will like this book.

★★   Not my cup of tea. Some people might enjoy it, but I cannot think of anyone!

★   Yawn! I cannot believe I read the whole thing.

The next three pages each contain three questions or writing prompts. Use these pages to record specific information, thoughts, and feelings as they relate to the questions. The questions are intended to help you think about different aspects of the book—those interesting, quirky, amusing things you might not consider before reading.

The last two blank pages for each book are intended as a place to record your ideas and reactions to the book. Here are some suggestions about how to use the blank pages.

• Record your thoughts and emotions as you read the book. Do any parts of the book evoke memories?

- Jot down quotes, phrases, and passages that grab your attention. You may want to share them with friends in the future.

- Are there any concepts in the book that you have trouble understanding? Are there any references with which you are not familiar? Take note of these concepts or references, and then look them up at your leisure.

- Write any questions that arise as you read the book. If the book is nonfiction, these questions may lead to further exploration about the topic in other books or sources. When you complete the book, you can look back and decide whether or not your questions were answered effectively.

- Jot down any of the book's strengths and weaknesses. For example, does the author of a fiction book have a strong sense of narrative style but leave some of the characters undeveloped? Are the facts in a nonfiction book strong, but the story itself or style of writing less than engaging?

You also can use the blank pages to answer some of the writing prompts listed below. (The questions have been divided into those for fiction and those for nonfiction.) If desired, support your answers with examples or passages from the book. These prompts are meant as starting points. Your own train of thought will lead you to "review" the book in your own unique way.

Fiction

- If you could live the life of one character in the book for a little while, who would it be and why?

- If you were a character in the book, what one thing would you do differently? How might this one action affect the rest of the book?
- If you could write a follow-up chapter or epilogue, what would it say?
- Did the book hold any surprises for you, or was the story line predictable?
- What do you think are the book's main themes? Is the author successful in getting these points across to the reader?
- How does the author present gender roles in the book?
- If the book were set in another time or place, how might it be different?
- How would you characterize relationships in the story? Are the relationships basically healthy, or are they mostly dysfunctional? Do the relationships improve by the end of the story?
- Imagine you are having coffee with one of the book's characters. What advice might you offer to that character?
- Is the story believable? Why or why not?
- Did the characters in the book remind you of any real-life acquaintances as you were reading?
- How does the author use foreshadowing? Is it subtle or obvious?
- If the book is one in a series, how does it measure up to the other books?
- Does the author use symbolism throughout the book? Is it effective?
- How does the author's use of language enhance the book?

- Does he or she use alliteration, metaphors, colloquialisms, or other tools to enliven the narrative?
- Does the author use mythological, religious, or literary imagery in the book? Does this enhance the story?
- Are you familiar with this author? Have you read any of his or her works before? If so, does his or her philosophy or view of life come through in the writing?
- What is the turning point in the story?
- In what way does the plot relate to your life today?

Nonfiction

- What did you know about the topic of the book before you started to read it? Did the book add to your knowledge or change your opinions about the subject?
- Did the book inspire you to take any action or learn more about its subject?
- If the book is a biography, how does the author feel about the person?
- After reading this book, would you agree that truth is stranger—and more interesting—than fiction?
- What other books have you read about the same topic? Compare this book with one of those. Which did you prefer and why? How do the authors treat the material? Do they present similar views or views that differ vastly? Do you feel that one covers the topic more completely than the other?
- Did you learn anything that you can utilize in your daily life by reading the book? Did you learn anything that you can

apply to your life in general?

- Do you think the book is an accurate and unbiased account? What are the author's credentials for writing such a book?
- If the author were paying a visit to your home for an afternoon, what questions would you want to ask him or her?

SUGGESTIONS FOR BOOK GROUP MEMBERS

The last section of this journal is provided to keep notes, recollections, and tidbits of information from book group meetings. The pages are designed for recording members' names and contact information. There also is space for comments and responses to the more interesting and provocative discussion points. Write your questions and comments prior to each meeting to prepare for the discussion. Shortly after each session, record your reflections and responses to the ideas presented during the meeting.

"Books, I have found, had the power to make time stand still, retreat or fly into the future" (Jim Bishop). Whether you are a member of an organized group or simply an avid reader, plan to enjoy the time you spend immersed in a good book!

A Good Book
Is the
Best of Friends

Book #1

Title: _Scenes at the Museum_
Author: _Kate Atkinson_
Genre: _____
Date of first publication: _____
Place of purchase: _____
Recommended by: ___ _MARIE_ _____
Recommended to: ___ _Book Club_ _____
Received as a gift from: _____
I chose to read this book because: _____
_____

1

_____
Favorite characters: _____
I would/~~would not~~ read other books by this author because: ___
The characters were well rounded
_____
_____
_____
~~Date lent~~: _____ ~~Date returned~~: _____
Book notes: _____
_____
_____
_____
_____
Rating: _____

Fiction

How realistic and well-developed are the main characters in the book? Do the characters interact with one another in a true-to-life manner?

Nonfiction

How important are the time period and setting to the subject matter? Could the events in the book have transpired in another time and place?

_____

_____

_____

_____

_____

_____

2 _____

_____

_____

_____

_____

_____

_____

_____

_____

_____

_____

_____

Fiction

Is the book's ending believable? Appropriate? Satisfying? Unsettling? Could the book have ended any other way? If you could rewrite the ending, what would you change?

Nonfiction

Were all of the questions raised in the story answered by the story's end? Were all of the loose ends tied up? Did the book make you want to read more books on the subject?

3

Fiction

Do you think that the book will be worth reading in ten years? How about in fifty years? Explain.

Nonfiction

Do you accept the author's presentation of the facts? What might his or her motivation have been to write the book? Do you believe that this motivation diminishes or strengthens the book?

4

_____

_____

_____

_____

_____

_____

_____

_____

_____

_____

_____

_____

_____

_____

_____

_____

_____

_____

Question: _____

_____

_____

5

Book #2

Title: _____

Author: _____

Genre: _____

Date of first publication: _____

Place of purchase: _____

Recommended by: _____

Recommended to: _____

Received as a gift from: _____

I chose to read this book because: _____

_____

_____

Favorite characters: _____

I would/would not read other books by this author because: ____

_____

_____

_____

_____

Date lent: _____ Date returned: _____

Book notes: _____

_____

_____

_____

_____

Rating: _____

Fiction

How realistic and well-developed are the main characters in the book? Do the characters interact with one another in a true-to-life manner?

Nonfiction

How important are the time period and setting to the subject matter? Could the events in the book have transpired in another time and place?

_____

_____

_____

_____

_____

_____

_____

_____

_____

_____

_____

_____

_____

_____

_____

_____

_____

_____

_____

Fiction

Is the book's ending believable? Appropriate? Satisfying? Unsettling? Could the book have ended any other way? If you could rewrite the ending, what would you change?

Nonfiction

Were all of the questions raised in the story answered by the story's end? Were all of the loose ends tied up? Did the book make you want to read more books on the subject?

_____

_____

_____

_____

_____

_____

_____

9

_____

_____

_____

_____

_____

_____

_____

_____

_____

_____

_____

Fiction

Do you think that the book will be worth reading in ten years? How about in fifty years? Explain.

Nonfiction

Do you accept the author's presentation of the facts? What might his or her motivation have been to write the book? Do you believe that this motivation diminishes or strengthens the book?

10

_____

_____

_____

_____

_____

_____

_____

_____

_____

_____

_____

_____

_____

_____

_____

_____

_____

_____

_____

Question: _____

_____

_____

_____

_____

_____

_____

_____

11

_____

_____

_____

_____

_____

_____

_____

_____

_____

_____

_____

_____

_____

Book #3

Title: _____

Author: _____

Genre: _____

Date of first publication: _____

Place of purchase: _____

Recommended by: _____

Recommended to: _____

Received as a gift from: _____

I chose to read this book because: _____

_____

_____

Favorite characters: _____

I would/would not read other books by this author because: ____

_____

_____

_____

_____

Date lent: _____ Date returned: _____

Book notes: _____

_____

_____

_____

_____

Rating: _____

13

Fiction

How realistic and well-developed are the main characters in the book? Do the characters interact with one another in a true-to-life manner?

Nonfiction

How important are the time period and setting to the subject matter? Could the events in the book have transpired in another time and place?

_____

_____

_____

_____

_____

_____

_____

_____

_____

_____

_____

_____

_____

_____

_____

_____

_____

_____

Fiction

Is the book's ending believable? Appropriate? Satisfying? Unsettling? Could the book have ended any other way? If you could rewrite the ending, what would you change?

Nonfiction

Were all of the questions raised in the story answered by the story's end? Were all of the loose ends tied up? Did the book make you want to read more books on the subject?

_____

_____

_____

_____

_____

_____

15

_____

_____

_____

_____

_____

_____

_____

_____

_____

_____

_____

Fiction

Do you think that the book will be worth reading in ten years? How about in fifty years? Explain.

Nonfiction

Do you accept the author's presentation of the facts? What might his or her motivation have been to write the book? Do you believe that this motivation diminishes or strengthens the book?

Question: _____

_____

_____

_____

_____

_____

_____

_____

17

_____

_____

_____

_____

_____

_____

_____

_____

_____

_____

_____

_____

Book #4

Title: _____

Author: _____

Genre: _____

Date of first publication: _____

Place of purchase: _____

Recommended by: _____

Recommended to: _____

Received as a gift from: _____

I chose to read this book because: _____

_____

_____

Favorite characters: _____

I would/would not read other books by this author because: _____

_____

_____

_____

_____

Date lent: _____ Date returned: _____

Book notes: _____

_____

_____

_____

_____

Rating: _____

Fiction

How realistic and well-developed are the main characters in the book? Do the characters interact with one another in a true-to-life manner?

Nonfiction

How important are the time period and setting to the subject matter? Could the events in the book have transpired in another time and place?

Fiction

Is the book's ending believable? Appropriate? Satisfying? Unsettling? Could the book have ended any other way? If you could rewrite the ending, what would you change?

Nonfiction

Were all of the questions raised in the story answered by the story's end? Were all of the loose ends tied up? Did the book make you want to read more books on the subject?

_____

_____

_____

_____

_____

_____

_____

21

_____

_____

_____

_____

_____

_____

_____

_____

_____

_____

_____

_____

Fiction

Do you think that the book will be worth reading in ten years? How about in fifty years? Explain.

Nonfiction

Do you accept the author's presentation of the facts? What might his or her motivation have been to write the book? Do you believe that this motivation diminishes or strengthens the book?

_____

_____

_____

_____

_____

_____

_____

_____

_____

_____

_____

_____

_____

_____

_____

_____

_____

_____

Question: _____

_____

_____

_____

_____

_____

_____

_____

_____

23

_____

_____

_____

_____

_____

_____

_____

_____

_____

_____

_____

_____

Book #5

Title: _____

Author: _____

Genre: _____

Date of first publication: _____

Place of purchase: _____

Recommended by: _____

Recommended to: _____

Received as a gift from: _____

I chose to read this book because: _____

_____

_____

Favorite characters: _____

I would/would not read other books by this author because: ____

_____

_____

_____

_____

Date lent: _____ Date returned: _____

Book notes: _____

_____

_____

_____

_____

Rating: _____

25

Fiction

How realistic and well-developed are the main characters in the book? Do the characters interact with one another in a true-to-life manner?

Nonfiction

How important are the time period and setting to the subject matter? Could the events in the book have transpired in another time and place?

_____

_____

_____

_____

_____

_____

_____

_____

_____

_____

_____

_____

_____

_____

_____

_____

_____

_____

Fiction

Is the book's ending believable? Appropriate? Satisfying? Unsettling? Could the book have ended any other way? If you could rewrite the ending, what would you change?

Nonfiction

Were all of the questions raised in the story answered by the story's end? Were all of the loose ends tied up? Did the book make you want to read more books on the subject?

Fiction

Do you think that the book will be worth reading in ten years? How about in fifty years? Explain.

Nonfiction

Do you accept the author's presentation of the facts? What might his or her motivation have been to write the book? Do you believe that this motivation diminishes or strengthens the book?

Question: _____

_____

_____

_____

_____

_____

_____

_____

_____

29

_____

_____

_____

_____

_____

_____

_____

_____

_____

_____

_____

_____

Book #6

Title: _____

Author: _____

Genre: _____

Date of first publication: _____

Place of purchase: _____

Recommended by: _____

Recommended to: _____

Received as a gift from: _____

I chose to read this book because: _____

_____

_____

Favorite characters: _____

I would/would not read other books by this author because: ____

_____

_____

_____

_____

Date lent: _____ Date returned: _____

Book notes: _____

_____

_____

_____

_____

Rating: _____

Fiction

How realistic and well-developed are the main characters in the book? Do the characters interact with one another in a true-to-life manner?

Nonfiction

How important are the time period and setting to the subject matter? Could the events in the book have transpired in another time and place?

_____

_____

_____

_____

Fiction

Is the book's ending believable? Appropriate? Satisfying? Unsettling? Could the book have ended any other way? If you could rewrite the ending, what would you change?

Nonfiction

Were all of the questions raised in the story answered by the story's end? Were all of the loose ends tied up? Did the book make you want to read more books on the subject?

_____

_____

_____

_____

_____

_____

_____

_____

_____

_____

_____

_____

_____

_____

_____

_____

_____

_____

_____

_____

Fiction

Do you think that the book will be worth reading in ten years? How about in fifty years? Explain.

Nonfiction

Do you accept the author's presentation of the facts? What might his or her motivation have been to write the book? Do you believe that this motivation diminishes or strengthens the book?

34

_____

_____

_____

_____

_____

_____

_____

_____

_____

_____

_____

_____

_____

_____

_____

_____

_____

_____

_____

Question: _____

_____

_____

_____

_____

_____

_____

_____

_____

35

_____

_____

_____

_____

_____

_____

_____

_____

_____

_____

_____

Book #7

Title: _____

Author: _____

Genre: _____

Date of first publication: _____

Place of purchase: _____

Recommended by: _____

Recommended to: _____

Received as a gift from: _____

I chose to read this book because: _____

_____

_____

Favorite characters: _____

I would/would not read other books by this author because: ___

_____

_____

_____

_____

Date lent: _____ Date returned: _____

Book notes: _____

_____

_____

_____

_____

Rating: _____

Fiction

How realistic and well-developed are the main characters in the book? Do the characters interact with one another in a true-to-life manner?

Nonfiction

How important are the time period and setting to the subject matter? Could the events in the book have transpired in another time and place?

Fiction

Is the book's ending believable? Appropriate? Satisfying? Unsettling? Could the book have ended any other way? If you could rewrite the ending, what would you change?

Nonfiction

Were all of the questions raised in the story answered by the story's end? Were all of the loose ends tied up? Did the book make you want to read more books on the subject?

_____

_____

_____

_____

_____

_____

39

_____

_____

_____

_____

_____

_____

_____

_____

_____

_____

_____

Fiction

Do you think that the book will be worth reading in ten years? How about in fifty years? Explain.

Nonfiction

Do you accept the author's presentation of the facts? What might his or her motivation have been to write the book? Do you believe that this motivation diminishes or strengthens the book?

_____

_____

_____

_____

_____

_____

_____

_____

_____

_____

_____

_____

_____

_____

_____

_____

_____

Question: _____

_____

_____

_____

_____

_____

_____

_____

_____

_____

_____

_____

_____

_____

_____

_____

_____

_____

_____

_____

_____

Book #8

Title: _____

Author: _____

Genre: _____

Date of first publication: _____

Place of purchase: _____

Recommended by: _____

Recommended to: _____

Received as a gift from: _____

I chose to read this book because: _____

_____

_____

Favorite characters: _____

I would/would not read other books by this author because: ____

_____

_____

_____

_____

Date lent: _____ Date returned: _____

Book notes: _____

_____

_____

_____

_____

Rating: _____

Fiction

How realistic and well-developed are the main characters in the book? Do the characters interact with one another in a true-to-life manner?

Nonfiction

How important are the time period and setting to the subject matter? Could the events in the book have transpired in another time and place?

_____

_____

_____

_____

_____

44

_____

_____

_____

_____

_____

_____

_____

_____

_____

_____

_____

_____

Fiction

Is the book's ending believable? Appropriate? Satisfying? Unsettling? Could the book have ended any other way? If you could rewrite the ending, what would you change?

Nonfiction

Were all of the questions raised in the story answered by the story's end? Were all of the loose ends tied up? Did the book make you want to read more books on the subject?

_____

_____

_____

_____

_____

_____

45

_____

_____

_____

_____

_____

_____

_____

_____

_____

_____

_____

Fiction

Do you think that the book will be worth reading in ten years? How about in fifty years? Explain.

Nonfiction

Do you accept the author's presentation of the facts? What might his or her motivation have been to write the book? Do you believe that this motivation diminishes or strengthens the book?

_____

_____

_____

_____

_____

_____

_____

_____

_____

_____

_____

_____

_____

_____

_____

_____

_____

_____

_____

_____

Question: _____

_____

_____

_____

_____

_____

_____

_____

_____

47

_____

_____

_____

_____

_____

_____

_____

_____

_____

_____

_____

_____

_____

Book #9

Title: _____

Author: _____

Genre: _____

Date of first publication: _____

Place of purchase: _____

Recommended by: _____

Recommended to: _____

Received as a gift from: _____

I chose to read this book because: _____

_____

_____

Favorite characters: _____

I would/would not read other books by this author because: ____

_____

_____

_____

_____

Date lent: _____ Date returned: _____

Book notes: _____

_____

_____

_____

_____

Rating: _____

Fiction

How realistic and well-developed are the main characters in the book? Do the characters interact with one another in a true-to-life manner?

Nonfiction

How important are the time period and setting to the subject matter? Could the events in the book have transpired in another time and place?

_____

_____

_____

_____

_____

_____

50

_____

_____

_____

_____

_____

_____

_____

_____

_____

_____

_____

_____

Fiction

Is the book's ending believable? Appropriate? Satisfying? Unsettling? Could the book have ended any other way? If you could rewrite the ending, what would you change?

Nonfiction

Were all of the questions raised in the story answered by the story's end? Were all of the loose ends tied up? Did the book make you want to read more books on the subject?

_____

_____

_____

_____

_____

_____

51

_____

_____

_____

_____

_____

_____

_____

_____

_____

_____

_____

Fiction

Do you think that the book will be worth reading in ten years? How about in fifty years? Explain.

Nonfiction

Do you accept the author's presentation of the facts? What might his or her motivation have been to write the book? Do you believe that this motivation diminishes or strengthens the book?

_____

_____

_____

_____

_____

_____

_____

_____

_____

_____

_____

_____

_____

_____

_____

_____

_____

_____

_____

Question: _____

_____

_____

53

Book #10

Title: _____

Author: _____

Genre: _____

Date of first publication: _____

Place of purchase: _____

Recommended by: _____

Recommended to: _____

Received as a gift from: _____

I chose to read this book because: _____

_____

_____

Favorite characters: _____

I would/would not read other books by this author because: ____

_____

_____

_____

_____

Date lent: _____ Date returned: _____

Book notes: _____

_____

_____

_____

_____

Rating: _____

Fiction

How realistic and well-developed are the main characters in the book? Do the characters interact with one another in a true-to-life manner?

Nonfiction

How important are the time period and setting to the subject matter? Could the events in the book have transpired in another time and place?

_____

_____

_____

_____

_____

_____

_____

_____

_____

_____

_____

_____

_____

_____

_____

_____

_____

_____

Fiction

Is the book's ending believable? Appropriate? Satisfying? Unsettling? Could the book have ended any other way? If you could rewrite the ending, what would you change?

Nonfiction

Were all of the questions raised in the story answered by the story's end? Were all of the loose ends tied up? Did the book make you want to read more books on the subject?

_____

_____

_____

_____

_____

_____

_____

57

_____

_____

_____

_____

_____

_____

_____

_____

_____

_____

_____

_____

Fiction

Do you think that the book will be worth reading in ten years? How about in fifty years? Explain.

Nonfiction

Do you accept the author's presentation of the facts? What might his or her motivation have been to write the book? Do you believe that this motivation diminishes or strengthens the book?

58

_____

_____

_____

_____

_____

_____

_____

_____

_____

_____

_____

_____

_____

_____

_____

_____

_____

_____

Question: _____

_____

_____

_____

_____

_____

_____

_____

59

_____

_____

_____

_____

_____

_____

_____

_____

_____

_____

_____

Book #11

Title: _____

Author: _____

Genre: _____

Date of first publication: _____

Place of purchase: _____

Recommended by: _____

Recommended to: _____

Received as a gift from: _____

I chose to read this book because: _____

_____

_____

Favorite characters: _____

I would/would not read other books by this author because: ___

_____

_____

_____

_____

Date lent: _____ Date returned: _____

Book notes: _____

_____

_____

_____

_____

Rating: _____

Fiction

How realistic and well-developed are the main characters in the book? Do the characters interact with one another in a true-to-life manner?

Nonfiction

How important are the time period and setting to the subject matter? Could the events in the book have transpired in another time and place?

_____
_____
_____
_____
_____
_____
_____
_____
_____
_____
_____
_____
_____
_____
_____
_____
_____
_____
_____

Fiction

Is the book's ending believable? Appropriate? Satisfying? Unsettling? Could the book have ended any other way? If you could rewrite the ending, what would you change?

Nonfiction

Were all of the questions raised in the story answered by the story's end? Were all of the loose ends tied up? Did the book make you want to read more books on the subject?

_____

_____

_____

_____

_____

_____

63

_____

_____

_____

_____

_____

_____

_____

_____

_____

_____

_____

_____

Fiction

Do you think that the book will be worth reading in ten years? How about in fifty years? Explain.

Nonfiction

Do you accept the author's presentation of the facts? What might his or her motivation have been to write the book? Do you believe that this motivation diminishes or strengthens the book?

Question: _____

_____

_____

_____

_____

_____

_____

_____

_____

_____

_____

_____

_____

_____

_____

_____

_____

_____

_____

_____

Book #12

Title: _____

Author: _____

Genre: _____

Date of first publication: _____

Place of purchase: _____

Recommended by: _____

Recommended to: _____

Received as a gift from: _____

I chose to read this book because: _____

_____

67

_____

Favorite characters: _____

I would/would not read other books by this author because: ____

_____

_____

_____

_____

Date lent: _____ Date returned: _____

Book notes: _____

_____

_____

_____

_____

Rating: _____

Fiction

How realistic and well-developed are the main characters in the book? Do the characters interact with one another in a true-to-life manner?

Nonfiction

How important are the time period and setting to the subject matter? Could the events in the book have transpired in another time and place?

_____
_____
_____
_____
_____

_____
_____
_____
_____
_____
_____
_____
_____
_____
_____
_____
_____

Fiction

Is the book's ending believable? Appropriate? Satisfying? Unsettling? Could the book have ended any other way? If you could rewrite the ending, what would you change?

Nonfiction

Were all of the questions raised in the story answered by the story's end? Were all of the loose ends tied up? Did the book make you want to read more books on the subject?

_____

_____

_____

_____

_____

_____ 69

_____

_____

_____

_____

_____

_____

_____

_____

_____

_____

_____

Fiction

Do you think that the book will be worth reading in ten years? How about in fifty years? Explain.

Nonfiction

Do you accept the author's presentation of the facts? What might his or her motivation have been to write the book? Do you believe that this motivation diminishes or strengthens the book?

Question: _____

_____

_____

_____

_____

_____

_____

_____

_____

71

_____

_____

_____

_____

_____

_____

_____

_____

_____

_____

_____

_____

Book #13

Title: _____

Author: _____

Genre: _____

Date of first publication: _____

Place of purchase: _____

Recommended by: _____

Recommended to: _____

Received as a gift from: _____

I chose to read this book because: _____

_____

_____

73

Favorite characters: _____

I would/would not read other books by this author because: ____

_____

_____

_____

_____

Date lent: _____ Date returned: _____

Book notes: _____

_____

_____

_____

_____

Rating: _____

Fiction

How realistic and well-developed are the main characters in the book? Do the characters interact with one another in a true-to-life manner?

Nonfiction

How important are the time period and setting to the subject matter? Could the events in the book have transpired in another time and place?

_____

_____

_____

_____

_____

_____

_____

_____

_____

_____

_____

_____

_____

_____

_____

_____

_____

_____

_____

Fiction

Is the book's ending believable? Appropriate? Satisfying? Unsettling? Could the book have ended any other way? If you could rewrite the ending, what would you change?

Nonfiction

Were all of the questions raised in the story answered by the story's end? Were all of the loose ends tied up? Did the book make you want to read more books on the subject?

_____

_____

_____

_____

_____

_____

75

_____

_____

_____

_____

_____

_____

_____

_____

_____

_____

_____

_____

Fiction

Do you think that the book will be worth reading in ten years? How about in fifty years? Explain.

Nonfiction

Do you accept the author's presentation of the facts? What might his or her motivation have been to write the book? Do you believe that this motivation diminishes or strengthens the book?

_____

_____

_____

_____

_____

_____

_____

_____

_____

_____

_____

_____

_____

_____

_____

_____

_____

_____

77

Book #14

Title: _____

Author: _____

Genre: _____

Date of first publication: _____

Place of purchase: _____

Recommended by: _____

Recommended to: _____

Received as a gift from: _____

I chose to read this book because: _____

_____

_____

79

Favorite characters: _____

I would/would not read other books by this author because: ___

_____

_____

_____

_____

Date lent: _____ Date returned: _____

Book notes: _____

_____

_____

_____

_____

Rating: _____

Fiction

How realistic and well-developed are the main characters in the book? Do the characters interact with one another in a true-to-life manner?

Nonfiction

How important are the time period and setting to the subject matter? Could the events in the book have transpired in another time and place?

_____

_____

_____

_____

_____

_____

_____

_____

_____

_____

_____

_____

_____

_____

_____

_____

_____

_____

Fiction

Is the book's ending believable? Appropriate? Satisfying? Unsettling? Could the book have ended any other way? If you could rewrite the ending, what would you change?

Nonfiction

Were all of the questions raised in the story answered by the story's end? Were all of the loose ends tied up? Did the book make you want to read more books on the subject?

Fiction

Do you think that the book will be worth reading in ten years? How about in fifty years? Explain.

Nonfiction

Do you accept the author's presentation of the facts? What might his or her motivation have been to write the book? Do you believe that this motivation diminishes or strengthens the book?

Question: _____

_____

_____

_____
_____
_____
_____
_____
_____
_____
_____
_____
_____
_____
_____
_____
_____
_____
_____
_____
_____
_____

Book #15

Title: _____

Author: _____

Genre: _____

Date of first publication: _____

Place of purchase: _____

Recommended by: _____

Recommended to: _____

Received as a gift from: _____

I chose to read this book because: _____

_____

_____

Favorite characters: _____

I would/would not read other books by this author because: ___

_____

_____

_____

_____

Date lent: _____ Date returned: _____

Book notes: _____

_____

_____

_____

_____

Rating: _____

Fiction

How realistic and well-developed are the main characters in the book? Do the characters interact with one another in a true-to-life manner?

Nonfiction

How important are the time period and setting to the subject matter? Could the events in the book have transpired in another time and place?

_____

_____

_____

_____

_____

_____

_____

_____

_____

_____

_____

_____

_____

_____

_____

_____

_____

Fiction

Is the book's ending believable? Appropriate? Satisfying? Unsettling? Could the book have ended any other way? If you could rewrite the ending, what would you change?

Nonfiction

Were all of the questions raised in the story answered by the story's end? Were all of the loose ends tied up? Did the book make you want to read more books on the subject?

_____

_____

_____

_____

_____

87

_____

_____

_____

_____

_____

_____

_____

_____

_____

_____

Fiction

Do you think that the book will be worth reading in ten years? How about in fifty years? Explain.

Nonfiction

Do you accept the author's presentation of the facts? What might his or her motivation have been to write the book? Do you believe that this motivation diminishes or strengthens the book?

Question: _____

_____

_____

_____

_____

_____

_____

_____

_____

_____

_____

_____

_____

_____

_____

_____

_____

_____

_____

_____

Book #16

Title: _____

Author: _____

Genre: _____

Date of first publication: _____

Place of purchase: _____

Recommended by: _____

Recommended to: _____

Received as a gift from: _____

I chose to read this book because: _____

_____

_____

Favorite characters: _____

I would/would not read other books by this author because: ____

_____

_____

_____

_____

Date lent: _____ Date returned: _____

Book notes: _____

_____

_____

_____

_____

Rating: _____

Fiction

How realistic and well-developed are the main characters in the book? Do the characters interact with one another in a true-to-life manner?

Nonfiction

How important are the time period and setting to the subject matter? Could the events in the book have transpired in another time and place?

_____

_____

_____

_____

_____

_____

_____

_____

_____

_____

_____

_____

_____

_____

_____

_____

_____

_____

Fiction

Is the book's ending believable? Appropriate? Satisfying? Unsettling? Could the book have ended any other way? If you could rewrite the ending, what would you change?

Nonfiction

Were all of the questions raised in the story answered by the story's end? Were all of the loose ends tied up? Did the book make you want to read more books on the subject?

_____

_____

_____

_____

_____

_____

93

_____

_____

_____

_____

_____

_____

_____

_____

_____

_____

_____

Fiction

Do you think that the book will be worth reading in ten years? How about in fifty years? Explain.

Nonfiction

Do you accept the author's presentation of the facts? What might his or her motivation have been to write the book? Do you believe that this motivation diminishes or strengthens the book?

_____

_____

_____

_____

_____

_____

_____

_____

_____

_____

_____

_____

_____

_____

_____

_____

_____

_____

Question: _____

_____

_____

_____

_____

_____

_____

_____

_____

_____

95

_____

_____

_____

_____

_____

_____

_____

_____

_____

_____

_____

_____

Book #17

Title: _____

Author: _____

Genre: _____

Date of first publication: _____

Place of purchase: _____

Recommended by: _____

Recommended to: _____

Received as a gift from: _____

I chose to read this book because: _____

_____

_____

Favorite characters: _____

I would/would not read other books by this author because: ____

_____

_____

_____

_____

Date lent: _____ Date returned: _____

Book notes: _____

_____

_____

_____

Rating: _____

Fiction

How realistic and well-developed are the main characters in the book? Do the characters interact with one another in a true-to-life manner?

Nonfiction

How important are the time period and setting to the subject matter? Could the events in the book have transpired in another time and place?

_____
_____
_____
_____
_____

_____
_____
_____
_____
_____
_____
_____
_____
_____
_____
_____
_____
_____

Fiction

Is the book's ending believable? Appropriate? Satisfying? Unsettling? Could the book have ended any other way? If you could rewrite the ending, what would you change?

Nonfiction

Were all of the questions raised in the story answered by the story's end? Were all of the loose ends tied up? Did the book make you want to read more books on the subject?

_____

_____

_____

_____

_____

_____

99

_____

_____

_____

_____

_____

_____

_____

_____

_____

_____

Fiction

Do you think that the book will be worth reading in ten years? How about in fifty years? Explain.

Nonfiction

Do you accept the author's presentation of the facts? What might his or her motivation have been to write the book? Do you believe that this motivation diminishes or strengthens the book?

_____

_____

_____

_____

_____

_____

_____

_____

_____

_____

_____

_____

_____

_____

_____

_____

_____

_____

Question: _____

_____

_____

_____

_____

_____

_____

_____

_____

101

_____

_____

_____

_____

_____

_____

_____

_____

_____

_____

_____

Book #18

Title: _____

Author: _____

Genre: _____

Date of first publication: _____

Place of purchase: _____

Recommended by: _____

Recommended to: _____

Received as a gift from: _____

I chose to read this book because: _____

_____

_____

Favorite characters: _____

I would/would not read other books by this author because: ____

_____

_____

_____

_____

Date lent: _____ Date returned: _____

Book notes: _____

_____

_____

_____

_____

Rating: _____

Fiction

How realistic and well-developed are the main characters in the book? Do the characters interact with one another in a true-to-life manner?

Nonfiction

How important are the time period and setting to the subject matter? Could the events in the book have transpired in another time and place?

_____

_____

_____

_____

_____

_____

_____

_____

_____

_____

_____

_____

_____

_____

_____

_____

_____

_____

Fiction

Is the book's ending believable? Appropriate? Satisfying? Unsettling? Could the book have ended any other way? If you could rewrite the ending, what would you change?

Nonfiction

Were all of the questions raised in the story answered by the story's end? Were all of the loose ends tied up? Did the book make you want to read more books on the subject?

_____

_____

_____

_____

_____

_____

105

_____

_____

_____

_____

_____

_____

_____

_____

_____

_____

_____

Fiction

Do you think that the book will be worth reading in ten years? How about in fifty years? Explain.

Nonfiction

Do you accept the author's presentation of the facts? What might his or her motivation have been to write the book? Do you believe that this motivation diminishes or strengthens the book?

Question: _____

_____

_____

_____

_____

_____

_____

_____

107

_____

_____

_____

_____

_____

_____

_____

_____

_____

_____

_____

Book #19

Title: _____

Author: _____

Genre: _____

Date of first publication: _____

Place of purchase: _____

Recommended by: _____

Recommended to: _____

Received as a gift from: _____

I chose to read this book because: _____

_____

_____

Favorite characters: _____

I would/would not read other books by this author because: ____

_____

_____

_____

_____

Date lent: _____ Date returned: _____

Book notes: _____

_____

_____

_____

Rating: _____

Fiction

How realistic and well-developed are the main characters in the book? Do the characters interact with one another in a true-to-life manner?

Nonfiction

How important are the time period and setting to the subject matter? Could the events in the book have transpired in another time and place?

_____
_____
_____
_____
_____
_____
110
_____
_____
_____
_____
_____
_____
_____
_____
_____
_____
_____
_____
_____

Fiction

Is the book's ending believable? Appropriate? Satisfying? Unsettling? Could the book have ended any other way? If you could rewrite the ending, what would you change?

Nonfiction

Were all of the questions raised in the story answered by the story's end? Were all of the loose ends tied up? Did the book make you want to read more books on the subject?

_____

_____

_____

_____

_____

_____

_____

_____

_____

_____

_____

_____

_____

_____

_____

_____

_____

_____

Fiction

Do you think that the book will be worth reading in ten years? How about in fifty years? Explain.

Nonfiction

Do you accept the author's presentation of the facts? What might his or her motivation have been to write the book? Do you believe that this motivation diminishes or strengthens the book?

Question: _____

_____

_____

_____
_____
_____
_____
_____
_____
113
_____
_____
_____
_____
_____
_____
_____
_____
_____
_____
_____
_____

Book #20

Title: _____

Author: _____

Genre: _____

Date of first publication: _____

Place of purchase: _____

Recommended by: _____

Recommended to: _____

Received as a gift from: _____

I chose to read this book because: _____

_____

_____

Favorite characters: _____

I would/would not read other books by this author because: ___

_____

_____

_____

_____

Date lent: _____ Date returned: _____

Book notes: _____

_____

_____

_____

_____

Rating: _____

Fiction

How realistic and well-developed are the main characters in the book? Do the characters interact with one another in a true-to-life manner?

Nonfiction

How important are the time period and setting to the subject matter? Could the events in the book have transpired in another time and place?

Fiction

Is the book's ending believable? Appropriate? Satisfying? Unsettling? Could the book have ended any other way? If you could rewrite the ending, what would you change?

Nonfiction

Were all of the questions raised in the story answered by the story's end? Were all of the loose ends tied up? Did the book make you want to read more books on the subject?

117

_____

_____

_____

_____

_____

_____

_____

_____

_____

_____

_____

_____

_____

_____

_____

_____

_____

_____

_____

Fiction

Do you think that the book will be worth reading in ten years? How about in fifty years? Explain.

Nonfiction

Do you accept the author's presentation of the facts? What might his or her motivation have been to write the book? Do you believe that this motivation diminishes or strengthens the book?

_____

_____

_____

_____

_____

_____

_____

_____

_____

_____

_____

_____

_____

_____

_____

_____

_____

Question: _____

_____

_____

_____

_____

_____

_____

_____

_____

_____

_____

_____

_____

_____

_____

_____

_____

_____

_____

_____

_____

_____

_____

Book #21

Title: _____

Author: _____

Genre: _____

Date of first publication: _____

Place of purchase: _____

Recommended by: _____

Recommended to: _____

Received as a gift from: _____

I chose to read this book because: _____

_____

_____

Favorite characters: _____

I would/would not read other books by this author because: ____

_____

_____

_____

_____

Date lent: _____ Date returned: _____

Book notes: _____

_____

_____

_____

_____

Rating: _____

Fiction

How realistic and well-developed are the main characters in the book? Do the characters interact with one another in a true-to-life manner?

Nonfiction

How important are the time period and setting to the subject matter? Could the events in the book have transpired in another time and place?

_____

_____

_____

_____

_____

_____

_____

_____

_____

_____

_____

_____

_____

_____

_____

_____

_____

_____

Fiction

Is the book's ending believable? Appropriate? Satisfying? Unsettling? Could the book have ended any other way? If you could rewrite the ending, what would you change?

Nonfiction

Were all of the questions raised in the story answered by the story's end? Were all of the loose ends tied up? Did the book make you want to read more books on the subject?

_____

_____

_____

_____

_____

_____

123

_____

_____

_____

_____

_____

_____

_____

_____

_____

_____

_____

Fiction

Do you think that the book will be worth reading in ten years? How about in fifty years? Explain.

Nonfiction

Do you accept the author's presentation of the facts? What might his or her motivation have been to write the book? Do you believe that this motivation diminishes or strengthens the book?

_____

_____

_____

_____

_____

_____

_____

_____

_____

_____

_____

_____

_____

_____

_____

_____

_____

_____

Question: _____

_____

_____

_____

_____

_____

_____

_____

_____

_____

125

_____

_____

_____

_____

_____

_____

_____

_____

_____

_____

_____

_____

_____

Book #22

Title: _____

Author: _____

Genre: _____

Date of first publication: _____

Place of purchase: _____

Recommended by: _____

Recommended to: _____

Received as a gift from: _____

I chose to read this book because: _____

_____

_____

Favorite characters: _____

I would/would not read other books by this author because: ___

_____

_____

_____

_____

Date lent: _____ Date returned: _____

Book notes: _____

_____

_____

_____

_____

Rating: _____

Fiction

How realistic and well-developed are the main characters in the book? Do the characters interact with one another in a true-to-life manner?

Nonfiction

How important are the time period and setting to the subject matter? Could the events in the book have transpired in another time and place?

_____

_____

_____

_____

_____

_____

_____

_____

_____

_____

_____

_____

_____

_____

_____

_____

_____

_____

Fiction

Is the book's ending believable? Appropriate? Satisfying? Unsettling? Could the book have ended any other way? If you could rewrite the ending, what would you change?

Nonfiction

Were all of the questions raised in the story answered by the story's end? Were all of the loose ends tied up? Did the book make you want to read more books on the subject?

_____

_____

_____

_____

_____

_____

129

_____

_____

_____

_____

_____

_____

_____

_____

_____

_____

_____

_____

Fiction

Do you think that the book will be worth reading in ten years? How about in fifty years? Explain.

Nonfiction

Do you accept the author's presentation of the facts? What might his or her motivation have been to write the book? Do you believe that this motivation diminishes or strengthens the book?

Question: _____

_____

_____

131

Book #23

Title: _____

Author: _____

Genre: _____

Date of first publication: _____

Place of purchase: _____

Recommended by: _____

Recommended to: _____

Received as a gift from: _____

I chose to read this book because: _____

_____

_____

133

Favorite characters: _____

I would/would not read other books by this author because: ____

_____

_____

_____

_____

Date lent: _____ Date returned: _____

Book notes: _____

_____

_____

_____

Rating: _____

Fiction

How realistic and well-developed are the main characters in the book? Do the characters interact with one another in a true-to-life manner?

Nonfiction

How important are the time period and setting to the subject matter? Could the events in the book have transpired in another time and place?

_____

_____

_____

_____

_____

_____

_____

_____

_____

_____

_____

_____

_____

_____

_____

_____

_____

_____

Fiction

Is the book's ending believable? Appropriate? Satisfying? Unsettling? Could the book have ended any other way? If you could rewrite the ending, what would you change?

Nonfiction

Were all of the questions raised in the story answered by the story's end? Were all of the loose ends tied up? Did the book make you want to read more books on the subject?

135

Fiction

Do you think that the book will be worth reading in ten years? How about in fifty years? Explain.

Nonfiction

Do you accept the author's presentation of the facts? What might his or her motivation have been to write the book? Do you believe that this motivation diminishes or strengthens the book?

Question: _____

_____

_____

_____

_____

_____

_____

137

_____

_____

_____

_____

_____

_____

_____

_____

_____

_____

_____

_____

_____

Book #24

Title: _____

Author: _____

Genre: _____

Date of first publication: _____

Place of purchase: _____

Recommended by: _____

Recommended to: _____

Received as a gift from: _____

I chose to read this book because: _____

_____

_____

139

Favorite characters: _____

I would/would not read other books by this author because: ____

_____

_____

_____

_____

Date lent: _____ Date returned: _____

Book notes: _____

_____

_____

_____

_____

Rating: _____

Fiction

How realistic and well-developed are the main characters in the book? Do the characters interact with one another in a true-to-life manner?

Nonfiction

How important are the time period and setting to the subject matter? Could the events in the book have transpired in another time and place?

_____

_____

_____

_____

_____

_____

_____

_____

_____

_____

_____

_____

_____

_____

_____

_____

_____

_____

Fiction

Is the book's ending believable? Appropriate? Satisfying? Unsettling? Could the book have ended any other way? If you could rewrite the ending, what would you change?

Nonfiction

Were all of the questions raised in the story answered by the story's end? Were all of the loose ends tied up? Did the book make you want to read more books on the subject?

_____

_____

_____

141

Fiction

Do you think that the book will be worth reading in ten years? How about in fifty years? Explain.

Nonfiction

Do you accept the author's presentation of the facts? What might his or her motivation have been to write the book? Do you believe that this motivation diminishes or strengthens the book?

Question: _____

_____

_____

_____

_____

_____

_____

_____

143

_____

_____

_____

_____

_____

_____

_____

_____

_____

_____

_____

_____

_____

_____

_____

Book #25

Title: _____

Author: _____

Genre: _____

Date of first publication: _____

Place of purchase: _____

Recommended by: _____

Recommended to: _____

Received as a gift from: _____

I chose to read this book because: _____

_____

_____

Favorite characters: _____

I would/would not read other books by this author because: ___

_____

_____

_____

_____

Date lent: _____ Date returned: _____

Book notes: _____

_____

_____

_____

_____

Rating: _____

Fiction

How realistic and well-developed are the main characters in the book? Do the characters interact with one another in a true-to-life manner?

Nonfiction

How important are the time period and setting to the subject matter? Could the events in the book have transpired in another time and place?

_____

_____

_____

_____

_____

_____

_____

_____

_____

_____

_____

_____

_____

_____

_____

_____

Fiction

Is the book's ending believable? Appropriate? Satisfying? Unsettling? Could the book have ended any other way? If you could rewrite the ending, what would you change?

Nonfiction

Were all of the questions raised in the story answered by the story's end? Were all of the loose ends tied up? Did the book make you want to read more books on the subject?

_____

_____

_____

_____

_____

_____

147

_____

_____

_____

_____

_____

_____

_____

_____

_____

_____

_____

_____

Fiction

Do you think that the book will be worth reading in ten years?
How about in fifty years? Explain.

Nonfiction

Do you accept the author's presentation of the facts? What might
his or her motivation have been to write the book? Do you
believe that this motivation diminishes or strengthens the book?

_____

_____

_____

_____

_____

_____

_____

_____

_____

_____

_____

_____

_____

_____

_____

_____

_____

Question: _____

_____

_____

_____

_____

_____

_____

_____

_____

149

_____

_____

_____

_____

_____

_____

_____

_____

_____

_____

_____

_____

Book Group Notes

Notes: _____
_____
_____
_____
_____
_____
_____
_____

151

_____

Name: _____
Address: _____
Telephone: _____
Fax: _____
E-mail: _____

Name: _____
Address: _____
Telephone: _____
Fax: _____
E-mail: _____

Name: _____

Address: _____

Telephone: _____

Fax: _____

E-mail: _____

Name: _____

Address: _____

Telephone: _____

Fax: _____

E-mail: _____

Name: _____

Address: _____

Telephone: _____

Fax: _____

E-mail: _____

Name: _____

Address: _____

Telephone: _____

Fax: _____

E-mail: _____

Name: _____

Address: _____

Telephone: _____

Fax: _____

E-mail: _____

Name: _____
Address: _____
Telephone: _____
Fax: _____
E-mail: _____

Name: _____
Address: _____
Telephone: _____
Fax: _____
E-mail: _____

Name: _____
Address: _____
Telephone: _____
Fax: _____
E-mail: _____

Name: _____
Address: _____
Telephone: _____
Fax: _____
E-mail: _____

Name: _____
Address: _____
Telephone: _____
Fax: _____
E-mail: _____

About the Author

Robin Doak is a freelance writer who specializes in both fiction and nonfiction educational materials, ranging from elementary school to college levels. She is also an avid reader.

Natalie Goldberg is the author of *Writing Down the Bones, Wild Mind, Long Quiet Highway, Banana Rose, Living Color,* and *Thunder and Lightning.* She lives in Northern New Mexico and leads workshops on writing and Zen practice nationwide. Visit her website: www.nataliegoldberg.com